The Keys to Success II:
The Best is Yet to Come

Terry Sprouse, editor

Planeta Books, LLC
Tucson, Arizona

Copyright ©2018 by Terry Sprouse.

All rights reserved. Printed in the United States of America. Except as permitted under the United States Copyright act of 1976, no part of this book may be reproduced or transmitted in any form or by any means, electronic or mechanical, including photocopying, recording, or by any information storage or retrieval system, without written permission from the copyright holder, except for the inclusion of quotations in a review.

ISBN 978-0-9798566-9-3

This publication is designed to provide accurate and authoritative information in regard to the subject matter covered. It is provided with the understanding that neither the author nor the publisher is engaged in rendering legal, accounting or other professional services. If legal or other expert assistance is required, the services of a competent professional person should be sought.

Published by:
Planeta Books, LLC
Tucson, Arizona

For updates and more resources visit:

www.TerrySprouse.com

Letting go isn't giving up. The best is yet to come.

-- Mike Dooley

Contents

1. Create Your Happiness

'Tis the Season 8
    Sally Lanyon
Why You Should Think Positively 13
    William David Hopper
Never Judge a Book by its Cover 18
    Randy Casarez

2. Making a Difference

Turning Points 24
    Philip L. Schultz
Is the Past, Present Tense? 32
    Art Lohman
Why Did I Serve 44
    John Grand
No Worry, No Hurry 48
    Kristy Hopper

3. Embrace Your Dream

I Feel Like a Teenager at the Age of 50 54
    Dr. Awdhesh Singh
Urban Boatman: A Father's Day Memoir 60
    G.L. Smith
Embracing the Experience 65
    Ken Requard, M.D.

4. Compassion

What if we Humans came with Expiration Dates 76
    James Babcock
Places in the Heart 81
    Terry Sprouse

Author Biographies 85

1

Create Your Happiness

We first make our habits, then our habits make us.
Anon

'Tis the Season

Sally Lanyon

Holidays can be the best of times; they can be the worst of times. I'm going to tell you about one such holiday.

The only place I didn't want to spend Christmas one particular year was at home alone in Tucson. What I did know was that I wanted to be with Tom and Brian, my bedrock sons who had moved to San Francisco after college graduation. I would have preferred to get out of the country, to be in a totally different setting, away from "the normal."

Tom suggested Uruguay where he had been an American Field Service (AFS) exchange student. He knew his host family in Treinta y Tres would welcome us into their home. The idea was appealing, extremely appealing, but $1800 a person for plane fare was out of reach for all of our pocketbooks.

We settled for San Francisco. One quick flight for me from Tucson and there we were. Together. Mom. Both sons.

The three of us were relationally unencumbered at the time. Tom was flirting with a woman at work, but hadn't asked her out yet. Brian was on the brink of getting back together with his college sweetheart who had broken up with him to pursue a Jesuit mission for two years. I was the one seeking asylum from the holiday, the memories, the pain. Earlier that year my fiancé and I had spent a joyful day planning my move into his house. He left my place, stopped for groceries, and never completed the left turn onto a main thoroughfare to his house. A truck drove into the driver's side of his Mercedes. His body was still when I saw him in the Emergency Room where staff had tried vainly to revive him. He looked alive, unhurt. He didn't answer my cries or respond to my caresses.

I knew about grieving. I pulled on my experience as a hospice bereavement counselor. That fall I asked myself the question I used to ask survivors, "What are your plans for the holiday?" I knew it was important for people to have plans for those triggering events. I made my plans. I was ahead of the game. I was coping.

There I was in the Mission District of San Francisco on the second floor of a three-story walk up. One of Tom's roommates graciously took the futon in the living room so I could have my own room for the visit. It was a quiet place to escape from the constant activity of the apartment. It was an interior room. Windowless and with only one floor lamp, the room was not unlike the city's famous fog. It was easy to sleep in on that first Sunday I was there. When I finally joined the gathering group of young people, I asked if anyone wanted to go to church. There were no takers. I was relieved. Deep down, I wanted to be alone.

On a neighborhood walk the day before, I had noticed a church that reminded me of San Xavier del Bac in the desert south of Tucson. Whitewashed adobe. Looming towers on the front two corners. Old. Centuries old. The only difference was that San Francisco's Mission Delores was bounded by concrete sidewalks rather than desert.

That Sunday I walked the four blocks to Mission Delores, directing my eyes to the cracks in the sidewalk to look up only at the street signs to be able to trace my way home. It was sunny, my leather jacket ample to keep me warm. I walked up the short flight of steps to the entrance of the church. I chose a pew mid-way back from the altar on the right side of the sanctuary. I sat on the aisle. There was a man in front of me. No one beside me.

The priest began speaking. In Spanish. I was in the Spanish mass. My Spanish skills are minimal despite several years of Spanish classes. I thought about leaving. I did not want to waste my time. Remembering what a work colleague once explained, "In Spanish, there is no concept of wasting time, only spending time." I decided to "spend" my time staying in the mass. I hoped it would not be a "waste" of time.

At first, I strained to hear the words of the liturgist, trying to interpret into English. When I realized I was only catching a few words, I listened to the lilt of the language instead. I studied the building, the high rounded arches on the ceiling, the lower arches lining the side aisles, the sun coming through the vibrant colors of the stained glass windows. I listened to the choir. The sounds of the hymns were familiar even if the words weren't.

I studied the man in front of me. In his late fifties, early sixties, wearing a torn beige jacket. His hair needed combing. He could have been one of those men who occasionally slept on the steps in front of Tom's apartment. I stared at him as he stared at a wallet-sized photo of a pretty brunette women held in his left hand. I imagined him missing her with all his heart. I felt the same way about my fiancé. I missed him with all my heart.

In the background, I heard certain words over and over: "Maria," "Joseph," "Bebe Jesus." I thought about Mary holding her baby. The joy she must have felt. The joy I felt with the first time I held my own sons. I silently wished that in that moment in Mission Delores, I could feel the joy Mary felt. I didn't really pray to God, I just said to myself, "I wish I could feel Mary's joy."

As the mass ended, I took one last look around the church, then retraced my steps to the apartment. A late lunch was in progress with a group of my sons' friends, some I had known in Tucson. They invited me to join in. I did, but I didn't say much. My son Brian suddenly turned to me and said, "Ma, you're back."

That seemed obvious. I was back from church. "Yes," I answered.

"No, you're <u>back</u>," he said with emphasis on the last word.

He meant, "You are fully present. You are not in your haze." I had tried so hard to cope with my loss those six months. I had cried about my loss, I had written about it, I had talked to other people about it. I was taking it one day at a time, as the clichéd advice goes. I would have told you I was coping fairly well, even better than expected.

Brian was saying to me, "Mom, your depression has lifted." He could feel the difference in me. I could feel the difference in me.

I don't often pray for myself, usually it is for other people and situations. I wouldn't even say that when I wished to feel Mary's joy, that that was a prayer. But maybe God heard my wish as a prayer. Because certainly that wish, that prayer, was answered.

That Christmas holiday was the worst of times, and it was the best of times.

Why You Should Think Positively

William David Hopper, DTM

I was learning to scuba dive for the first time. After a week of classroom sessions covering the principles of the sport, I found myself in the pool with my entire class and a regulator in my mouth.

The instructor said, "It is time to go underwater for the first time."

We began to descend in unison.

Less than ten seconds after my head ~~goes~~ went below the surface of the water, I realized I could not take a breath. My mind told me taking a breath under water was not something humans should be doing. Humans cannot breathe under water.

I quickly shot up to the surface with real fear that I would drown.

We all have experienced situations in our lives when we have been afraid, and that fear has prevented us from accomplishing something we set out to do. Many of these fears stem from our perception of what people think of us. They come from peer pressure, from the desire to fit in, or the desire to not be embarrassed.

One hundred and fifty years from now, no one who knows you will be still be alive. Why does their perception or opinion even matter?

When an astronaut looks at the planet from the moon, you are nothing more than an unperceivable speck on the world.

The Earth itself is no more than a speck in the galaxy; the galaxy is no more than a speck in the universe. Which means that we amount to a speck on a speck on a speck.

I ask again, why does another person's perception matter to you? Many of you might be thinking it doesn't matter; you do not care what other people think. Although it may be a nice thought, it is probably not true.

Does the thought of standing in front of an audience of 500 people, all waiting to hear you give a five-minute speech, make you nervous?

Have you ever felt like you wanted to speak up and say something to someone? Maybe they were committing a crime or just being a jerk to someone.

Have you ever bought the popular brand or dressed a certain way, in order to fit in?

If you answered yes to any of the questions above, the uncomfortable truth is: the opinion of other people matters to you.

Olin Miller said, "You probably wouldn't worry about what people think of you if you could know how seldom they do."

The truth is people are the center of their own universe and you are merely a speck on a speck on a speck.

Now I know what you might be thinking: "That might sound good, but I have been at the mall and judged people as they walked by. I have been mad at people when they cut me off in traffic. I have been mad at servers when they got my order wrong."

You also might be thinking that as humans, we have more negative thoughts about people than positive thoughts.

I believe this is because negative thoughts are like high frequency radio waves. They can consume us in the moment but are generally short lived. Can you recall the details of the last person you judged at the mall? Do you remember the last person who cut you off or the last server who got your order wrong?

Several months ago, I received an instant message from a childhood bully. I was lucky because my bullies were rather uninspired and their bullying consisted mainly of 'name calling' and 'keep away'. Many people have suffered a lot worse when it comes to bullying.

This particular bully from my childhood wrote me to apologize for all the things he did to me. For the life of me, I could not remember who this person even was. He was a high frequency radio wave in my life. The great thing is even though negative thoughts are like high frequency radio waves, positive thoughts are more like low frequency radio waves. They might be over shadowed in the present but they are long lasting and long reaching.

Drew Dudley has a *TEDx* video titled "Leading with Lollipops." Drew talks about a time where he was handing out lollipops to new potential college students on a campus tour. He stopped and talked to a young new student, handed her a lollipop without thinking much about it.

Four years later, at another event, the same student approached Drew after he delivered a speech. She told him that four years earlier, following a tour of the campus, she was ready to tell her parents that college just wasn't the right choice for her, but when he gave her the lollipop, it changed her mind. She went on to say that she would be graduating soon and it was all due to him giving her the lollipop. While small negative actions are short lived, small positive actions can have long lasting effects.

My wife and I go all out when we decorate for Christmas every year. It takes us around five, 12 to 16 hour days to get everything up.

It is a lot of work and many years we ask ourselves, "Do we really want to spend the time and energy to do it?"

Part of the reason we do it, however, is because many of the neighbors enjoy the decorations. One neighbor in particular, takes their holiday card photos in front of our house.

My wife and I never really knew the full extent of how much our decorations meant to others until last year. After having our decorations up for a few weeks, my wife received a *Facebook* message from one of our neighbors. She described the pain seven years earlier of her divorce and how she had given up on Christmas and decorating. The pain of her divorce robbed her of the Christmas spirit because she felt like their house could never look like it used to. She went on to say our decorations, year after year, helped bring back the Christmas spirit in her heart.

She wrote, "You brighten the block for so many of us. I bet you never knew how important that was to me. So thank you."

No, we never knew.

Small positive acts can have life changing impacts.

When I started scuba diving, I almost let the fear of not being able to breathe under water stop me from learning one of my current favorite activities. When I decorated for Christmas, I almost let the work required stop me from renewing the Christmas spirit for my neighbor. In Toastmasters I mentor new members, helping them grow as individuals and leaders, which I would not be able to do if I gave into the fear of my very first speech.

I challenge you to not allow fear, worry of other's opinions, or hard work hold us back from the goals we want to accomplish. I challenge you to not allow small high frequency negative waves affect your goals. I challenge you to have the courage to create small low frequency positive waves.

Remember, no one you know will be alive in one hundred and fifty years, so do not give power to the opinions of others. You might not be alive or even be remembered, but by creating small low frequency positive waves, you can create your own personal "butterfly effect." You can affect someone in a positive way, who then affects someone else in a positive way.

You can create your own personal legacy. You can give someone a lollipop, you can change someone life.

Never Judge a Book by its Cover

Randy Casarez

When I was 9-years-old, I was diagnosed with a learning disability. When people think of learning disabilities, they think of *dyscalculia* (difficulty in making arithmetical calculations,), *dyslexia* (difficulty in learning to read), and of course *ADHD* (attention deficit hyperactivity disorder).

A learning disability is a disorder that interferes with a student's capacity to listen, think, speak, write, spell, or do mathematical calculations. Students who possess a specific learning disability may struggle with reading, writing, or math.

It's common for an individual to have a learning disability in one or two areas. It's not that common for an individual to have a disability in all three. I can honestly say that I do struggle in all three.

Every time, I meet someone new, they always make the same observation and ask me the same question.

"Randy, you look normal to me. What type of learning disability do you have?"

When I tell people that my learning disability is in math, reading, and writing. They look shocked. I always get the same follow up question.

"Randy, how did you graduate with four college degrees?"

Getting Through College

Well, it was not easy. For every written assignment that I had to complete in college, I would make sure to go to the writing tutor and have them help me with my grammar. Same thing with math, and all of my homework assignments. If I knew that I had a test coming up, I would do everything in my power to study for that test.

Even with all of the help that I received, I still continued to struggle. I was happy to get B's and C'S. My goal was to prove to people that no matter what type of disability you may have, you can still achieve your goals.

I want people to understand that just because you have a disability, it does not mean that you cannot have big dreams and have a successful life.

The key to achieving your goals is to know you're learning disability inside and out. Also, do not be afraid to fail.

I have learned that even though people may not think that I have a learning disability, I do have one. Sometimes people get upset, because I may not understand something right away. Part of my learning disability is being a little slow to grasp certain concepts. You may have to tell me 20 times, before I will understand.

I try to remind myself that I have a learning disability, and I need to be able to pace myself.

Sometimes I find myself getting upset. I ask God, "Why me?" Then, I always remind myself that it could be a lot worse.

My years in *Toastmasters* has taught me that there are other disabilities that are even more challenging. There are people in this world that cannot talk, or walk.

Flying Without Arms

There is a young lady, Jessica Cox, who was born with no arms and she was able to get her pilot license. Imagine having no arms. Jessica has every reason to feel sorry for herself, but she does not.

Instead she took her disability and made it work for her. I'm sure that when people see her they assume that she can't do anything, but Jessica always proves them wrong. She is pilot, and motivational speaker. She uses her feet, the way we would use our hands. She can open soda cans, and she can write.

I don't know Jessica, but I'm sure she had moments when she wanted to quit.

I imagine, something inside of her said,

"I'm not going to lay around feeling sorry for myself. I'm going to be successful, and determine my own path."

Strength From Disabilities

Most people who have disabilities are successful, because they do not let defeat get the best of them. They don't give up. They look at their disability not as an obstacle, but as a strength.

There is a stereotype that people with disabilities are lazy. There is also a misconception that disabilities are only physical.

Just because I'm not in wheelchair, does not mean I don't have a disability. Yes, I have a disability, and I am proud to have my learning disability.

Although it has been struggle, I would not change a thing. My learning disability has taught me what my strengths and my weakness are. I'm the type of person, that if I don't know the answer, I will find someone who does. I'm always willing to put 110% into anything I do. If I lose, then at least I can say I gave best effort

I'm proud that, even though I have learning disability in math, I was able to get master's degree in accounting. I'm proud that even though I have a hard time writing, I was able to write and publish a short story, "The Big Ones," and currently, I am writing my first official novel, "Hope Change Is In You."

I'm proud that even though I have a difficult time saying words, I was able to achieve success in *Toastmasters*. In my seven years of Toastmasters, I have been able to achieve two *Distinguished Toastmaster* awards, the highest honor in *Toastmasters*. It was not because I was a great leader. It was because I was willing to participate and give speeches as often as possible.

I achieved things not because I'm great but because I know who I am, and I know my strengths and weakness. Oh yeah, a little hard work and determination does not hurt at all. You have to be willing to put yourself out there.

So for those that don't know me, my name is Randy Casarez and I have a learning disability.

Never judge a book by its cover.

2
Making a Difference

If you want a happy ending, that depends, of course, on where you stop your story.

Orson Welles

*Turning Points

Philip L. Schultz
Colonel USAF (retired)

Turning points occur in everyone's life. Many occur every day. "What should I do next?" is a question we ask and answer over and over. I am glad I have a visual record of the major turning points in my life, starting with childhood memories.

At two years of age, my six year older brother and three year older sister were asked to put me in my crib with fancy cast iron bars. I went to climb out and they pushed me back down. So, I decided to pull up the bottom of the crib and crawl out, where upon I almost suffocated. Dad came to my rescue and put us in his lap on the front porch where I promptly fell asleep and was put back into my crib. You need to speak your mind and someone will usually help you out.

The next major change in my life was to become a kindergarten drop out. We moved to a suburb of Philadelphia in November and I started school at the Highland Park Elementary School. Brother John was in sixth grade, sister Ruth was in third grade and I was put in Kindergarten. I was happily learning and doing a crayon drawing when I apparently wasn't listening to my kindergarten teacher. She grabbed me under the shoulder and shook me. I cried and she threw me in the closet. When my siblings brought me home, my mother was so upset, she said kindergarten is a new idea and I could stay home. To cope with my boredom, she had me cut out appliances and furniture from a *Sears Roebuck Catalogue* and paste them in a notebook.

One day, I asked my mother where I came from. She said I came from her and my daddy and they came from their mothers and daddies all the way back to Adam and Eve, who God made in the beginning, and God has always existed. You can learn many things from your mother.

My next major turning point was taking over my brother's afternoon newspaper route for six years. I had an average of 70 customers for which I was paid one cent a paper per day. It taught me many things about people, and about being responsible.

I had to deliver papers on time every single day except for Sunday and two holidays. Dad sent the collected money to the newspaper. I got to keep 20 cents a week for myself and the rest went to help my brother and sister through college. Then, when it was my turn to go to college, they helped me. Having a job teaches you responsibility.

Next, I attended *Drexel Tech* in Philadelphia, which is now a University. I was in the Cooperative Engineering Program. After attending for three quarters I was required to work in an industry for six months out of the year, and write reports for myself. My employer also wrote reports about my work.

Being a Cooperative program I worked odd jobs and received union pay at the old refinery. In my junior year at Drexel, I was called into the *Army Air Corps*. Writing ratings on yourself in a cooperative program gives you real life job experience.

After basic training in the Army Air Corp in Florida, I soloed in the *P17 Stearman* Bi-plane there. At basic training in Alabama I went to fly one morning and found no airplanes to fly. The upper class had gone up at night without proper training or a full set of instruments and had spiraled into the ground. After a Congressional investigation it was determined that we would have a full set of instruments on all the time. My class of 1944 was the first class to graduate as cadets with instrument ratings which permitted us to fly in all kinds of weather. It's important to review what people need to learn.

As a Lt Pilot I flew gunnery missions in Florida for two months and then was sent to Massachusetts to meet my *B24 Liberator* crew for training. We picked up a new *Ford* built *B24J Liberator Bomber* and flew all the way from Newfoundland to the *Azores Islands* (in Portugal) where the weather turned below minimum altitude visibility of 100 feet.

The two planes ahead of us couldn't find the runway and crashed into a mountain, killing all but three of each crew. We found a break in the clouds and skimmed in over the Atlantic Ocean and landed on a blacked out airfield. All the lights were out to avoid enemy attacks. Although trained to do things one way, always put safety first and be flexible in what you do.

I flew 35 missions out of Italy, all over Eastern Europe. Once when flying over the Alps, near Linz, Austria, we bombed the *Herman Tank Factory*. Anti-aircraft fire was so severe it cut the control cable under the pilot seat and the pilot lost control of the airplane. He broadcast over the air that we were bailing out. I looked down over snow-covered Austria and knew that if I bailed out I would either freeze to death or be made a POW (prisoner of war).

The crew watching me from the front and back bulkheads was waiting for me to jump before they jumped out. I saw the auto pilot control and threw it in. The plane lurched. The pilot threw the auto pilot out again. I threw it back in and adjusted the controls and the plane came out of its dive.

We flew home safely and in the debriefing the general from headquarters said to my pilot, "I hear that your crew doesn't obey you. Put your copilot Lieutenant Philip Schultz in for a *Distinguished Flying Cross* and make him a first pilot." The *Distinguished Flying Cross* was the third highest award you could receive for valor in combat. Think out of the box and don't always obey orders.

On returning to the states, I ferried war weary B24s to *Davis Monthan Air Force Base* and flew new B24s to the west coast. Then, because of my experience and instrument rating, I transported urgently needed supplies and troops, until I was discharged. Experience and training makes a difference.

Once when I was stationed near Memphis, a *Red Cross* bus provided rides into town to go to a sorority house party. There was no food left when we got there and we were hungry so we invited the girls out to the hotel where there was dancing and food. The girl I had previously met already had a date, but she introduced me to another girl who agreed to go out with me. That was Sally, my future bride. When I took her home she taught me the *Camel Walk*, a new dance step.

Another time I had flown a plane to Dallas and there was no place to stay. I heard there was a plane going back to Memphis which was on the way to Nashville, my home base at that time. Sally met me in Memphis, escorted by her uncle Robert, and our romance blossomed. I communicated frequently with

Sally as I completed my Industrial Engineering degree at *Drexel University*. She flew up for my senior prom and to meet my parents.

Unfortunately she had quite a time getting up there as there was a storm near Philadelphia and she had to take a train from Washington DC to Philadelphia. We were overjoyed when we finally met at *Penn Station*. I could talk to Sally on an intellectual level where all the other girls only talked about music and dancing. She was gorgeous though and I remember that she wore an off the shoulder dress and was a good dancer. Communication with your spouse is one of the most important things in a marriage.

I was to be employed in 1946 at *Campbell Soup* when its president suddenly died. My sponsor said he couldn't hire me in till they hired a new president. My girlfriend's family in Memphis, Tennessee found me a good job there. I also joined the *Army Air Corp Reserve*. Since I was a Yankee in rebel land, the only place I felt I was treated as an equal was in the Army Air Corps Reserve as a pilot. It's important to be treated as an equal.

I was recalled involuntarily to active duty during the Korean War. My job was in the Air Corps flying *C46 Cargo Planes* and dropping Army paratroopers, with extra duty as Ground Training Officer and Personal Equipment Officer. I had my first daughter, but I had to leave my wife and daughter for a whole month dropping the army paratroopers. I was scheduled to go to graduate school at *Wright Patterson AFB* and my second daughter was born at that time, so I did not fly anymore in Korea. Education and children were important reasons for going into grad school.

When I entered grad school, a professor looked at my transcript and said "Drexel, you won't have any trouble here." Just after graduation from *Wright Patterson* our third daughter was born. I went into *Central Procurement* of aircraft ground power units and also power plant equipment such as diesel generators for power plants as far away as Saudi Arabia and Tripoli, Libya.

Then I became *Contracting Officer* at Grand Forks, North Dakota. One time the base commissary officer said we had no potatoes and I found out the potatoes were being shipped from North Dakota to Kansas City on the quarter master's order. I located a small business to buy the potatoes from, and from then on we always had potatoes.

In Topeka, Kansas we mud jacked (pumping a water, dirt and cement mixture under a concrete slab) the runway. I found that we could mud jack in our backyard and stopped the flooding into our basement. At *Forbes Air force* base in Topeka Kansas, I earned an award as Outstanding *Procurement Officer* of the Air Force.

I was *Cub Master* and Air Force *Boy Scout* project officer at the last two bases. I was in *Toastmasters* in Grand Forks and did speeches on flag courtesy, contracting, and flying. Each change of station was a turning point. This all shows the importance of following the *Boy Scout* oath "to serve my country and serve others."

We loved taking family taking vacations where ever I was stationed. One was a Mediterranean cruise where we had a cabin for eight and there were only five of us. We flew to Rome and drove all over Switzerland

and Germany and took trains from Venice and Rome to Sicily. We went to Germany and Switzerland several times and took a cog rail road up the *Zugspitze* (Germany's highest peak).

Upon returning to the United States, we went to the *New York World's Fair* and stayed at the *Waldorf Astoria* and wished we could have stayed there the entire time. There were seven of us in the car when we went to the *San Antonio World's Fair*. We went to *Montreal World's Fair* and continued on to Quebec. We went to *Air Force Spiritual Life Conferences* at Estes Park, Colorado and at Glorietta, North Carolina.

Visits from and to grandparents were always fun. We always made a point of eating together and praying before we eat. One way to have the girls participate was to have them bring something they learned at school to the table. We participated in church as Sunday school teachers, and singing in the choir. It's important to learn new things about our world and to learn how to help your family through spiritual growth.

On retirement, I ran a retirement home for a year and the spent 15 years selling life insurance at three military bases. We kept men who were just getting out of prison and also many missionaries and our pastor at our home, when they needed help. I also have been involved in *Reading Seed, Mops, Awana,* choir and Sunday school at my church.

I was honored in February 2018 by *One on One Partners* for caring for two boys from fifth grade up through high school, on a weekly basis. Both boys have earned scholarships to college. I loved to stay active and help children, in the same way that I helped my own children grow up.

My late wife and I would travel on our own, or with tours, to many countries. We attended *International Christian Businessmen Conventions* in Australia, the Philippines, Korea, South Africa and Scotland, as well as many in the US. We went on many *Road Scholar* trips to various places in Canada, Flagstaff, Chicago, San Diego, among others. Many trips were on our own to The Holy Land, Egypt, France, Scandinavian countries, Russia, South American countries, China, and India.

I was in a clown ministry in Tucson Called *Faithful Fools*. I always carried balloons with me to blow up and give to the children. I taught the minister in Saigon how to blow up balloons and he would ask for them every time he came to our church. We enjoyed visiting with our three children, two grandchildren and five great grandchildren. We always liked learning and sharing our faith!

At 97, in April of 2018, I am still active at church, the Air Force Base, *Toastmasters*, and the *Republican Club*. Now handicapped by worn out legs, I spend most of my time in a wheel chair at my cell phone and computer, and church. Currently, I have a missionary family of four from Brazil, who are here on a sabbatical before returning to Brazil in July of 2018. Again it is always important to stay active and share your faith.

We all have many turning points in our lives, which makes life a continuous adventure.

Enjoy it!

Don't ever quit!

Is the Past, Present Tense?
Art Lohman

History repeats
One more
Refuses to
Learn from

The above poem was written because much of the worlds' misery, that has occurred and is still occurring, could have been avoided. We are a prisoner of our past, if we do not use our gifts of memory, conscience and compassion. We must remember when we have wronged others. Our conscience tells us what we have done wrong and what we should then do to correct it. Compassion directs us to right our wrongs, when possible, and to change our treatment of others. As the Bible says, "Do to others as you would have them do to you." Though others may refuse to learn the lessons of history, we must remember them and act in accordance with what we know to be right.

In school, reading and writing were a struggle for me. I did not learn how to read until I was in the third grade. That school year alone, I was in four different schools. I was in two schools while my father was stationed at two Air Bases in England, and two more when he was stationed at *Charleston Air Force Base*, South Carolina.

One school was off base and the other on base, after we moved into base housing. Even as an adult, I experience not just problems in reading and writing, but often I have a difficult time retrieving information from memory, and I frequently act impulsively. At the age of forty-one at the *University of Utah*, I was found to have a learning disability.

Learning disabled people generally have average or higher intelligence. I believe the reason no one discovered my disability until then, was because I also possessed a vivid imagination.

As a member of my high school chess club, I created my own chess strategy. Before I made a move against opponents, the moved piece had to accomplish three things:

1) Defend my position;

2) Attack my opponent; and,

3) Not force me to retreat on my next move.

I also found ways to improve my skill by experimenting with my opponent during the game. Winning was not always my goal. When playing a more experienced player I wanted to learn from them.

As a teenager and an adult I felt different from those around me. I joined *Toastmasters International* to help me develop my speaking ability. I believe that writing poetry was another way for me to share who I am with others. Knowing that I am learning disabled, explains why, despite my difficulty in the learning process, I kept searching for different ways for me to learn.

As an actor I write my lines over and over until I can write them from memory. I should say I try to remember them, in order to write them down. This way when I am on stage, if I forget a word or two, I will still remember, in general, what I am to say.

When I started to write my poems, I had a dictionary at my side. As part of my disability, even when I spell words correctly, sometimes they don't look properly spelled to me. I also had a dictionary because I liked to see the definition of the words.

I believe my experiences as a child, moving from place to place, and as an adult with an invisible disability, influenced what I wrote and thought about. I seemed to have a perspective on life that came from left field. In many ways I am a mystery to myself.

In the summer of 1978, in Philadelphia, Pennsylvania, arsonists set fire to a building. While firefighters were fighting the fire, the arsonists were shooting at them. Several firefighters and police officers were wounded. One police officer died. I was driving back to *McGuire Air Force Base*, in New Jersey, where I worked and lived. On the radio, forty-one miles away from the fire, I heard about the shootings. I had to park the car, finding myself overwhelmed with emotion.

I could not imagine anyone shooting at those who were already putting their lives on the line. This fire, if it spread, could put the lives and livelihoods of others at risk. I knew what I had signed up for when I joined the military, but these firefighters and police officers were not soldiers. I felt compelled to write down my thoughts.

Admiration of a Firefighter

Honey, let's go for a drive, before work tonight.
It's been a beautiful day let's end it right.
A job I could do this night.
A job, one, cannot do without might.

Alarms Rang
Sirens Wailed
Flames grew hotter with each new height

Engulfed in hell, the firefighter dueled with Death.
Death stared at the firefighter and laughed, this is the night.
The firefighter, gasp one breath and died in the fight.

My next poem was written after domestic terrorists planted a bomb at the train station in Bologna, Italy, August 2nd 1982. When it exploded, over two hundred people were wounded and eighty-five killed. Seven of those killed ranged from the ages of three to sixteen. At the scene among the victims there was not one terrorist.

Tiny Hand

A tiny hand, upon the ground
At first I thought it broke off a doll
The red puddle it laid in told me different

Pieces of torn flesh and metal fragments
surrounded by puddles of red laid everywhere

On the evening news, I cried who could do such a thing?
A hundred groups shouted ***"Us"*** *in response*
"We Warriors for Peace fight and die for you the people"

But upon the cold, red ground
*Not one **"Warrior"** lies scattered amongst the fragments of the bomb wrecked train station*

    I wrote this poem in the early eighties. Years earlier Russia had sent troops into Afghanistan to support a puppet government. In Beirut, Lebanon, in 1983, two-truck bombs exploded outside a barracks, killing 241 American soldiers. There were several famines that had just occurred, or were occurring, in various African countries. In most of the world there was relative peace and prosperity. It seemed, you were either blessed or cursed, depending on where you were born or whom your parents were.

Reality

Birds flying
Bombs sailing

Fruits growing
Hunger pangs and moaning

Flowers blooming
Children dying

Population booming
Abortions abounding

Reality
A beautiful rose with a thorny stem

    In the seventies I was temporarily assigned to *Andrews Air Force Base*, now known as *Joint Base Andrews* in Maryland. While there, I met two enlisted aircrews from Chile, when their aircraft landed there. They told me that they had to wear black armbands, even in uniform, to show that they were loyal to the government. Later in the eighties mass graves were being discovered in several South American countries. Death Squads and in some cases government soldiers had killed innocent people and secretly buried them. Political opposition could mean the death penalty. Fortunately, in our country you are free to voice your opinions for or against our leaders

Free to Think

Heaved through the door, to the cells cold bare floor.
The crime, composing verses of rhyme that
spark the mind to wonderment, to question.

Few selected to Scribe Noblest
Wielding the power to influence minds.
Only those with divine intellect rise above.

Fallen from grace, no longer inspired.
Existence, officially erased from
social media, records of being.

Convicting words of blasphemy, treason
promoting autonomous judicious
thinking, confessed public manipulation.

Alone in the freezing dark with one more
subtle bruise. Ideas, struggle to live
inside a culture, of unwritten, rules.

Rolling over, staring up through the ceiling
Seeing stars freely lighting up darkness
Gives hope to an aimless, penitent scribe.

If the deaf could hear the truth, would they
refuse to see it? Even if. Blinded, I
hear, investigative, human nature.

Obligated to write desireless words for
a meaningless existence, is a life
sentence to a, slow, mediocre, death.

How many have I mislead? To even ask!
Is more excruciating then anything
than what they have done and will do to me.

Body, soul drained, heavy weary eyelids weigh shut.
Blaring sounds suddenly erupt in the cell..
Floodlights burn though bars, eyelids. Rest snatched.

Sleep no longer refuge for sanity.
Hour after hour clamorous, turbulent din
obtrusive lights, permeates the stale air.

Years of endless days blurs vision, deafens
senses, numbs the mind. Miraculously
an ember of an idea smolders, dreams.

Will, unwilling to bend or surrender,
believing in an illusion, safer.
Schooled to except, discernment discouraged.

My words once herald the path to follow.
Building upon a foundation, engineered
constructed by ruminating agents.

Confounded by naysayers, deniers.
Perfection of humanity, all should seek.
Citizens, useful tools, in the right hands.

Sculpting a new society from old,
is a process of elimination.
Removing obsolete customs, beliefs.

Imagine a world in sync, with one creed.
No room in a conforming society
for dissention. Reflection forbidden.

I did what it took to ascend the ladder.
The task before me arduous, pleasing
Hailed as the king of words, not courts jester!

Believing what I wrote helped convince others.
Protégés, politically zealous,
Climbing, challenging, pushing status quo.

Déjà vu triggered by reality
As a child I dreamed, of a better world.
Do children still dream of a better world?

Blacksmiths forge metal into shapes they desire.
People not molded from dreams of others.
I needed to see this, though a child's eyes.

My folly, condemns me, my thoughts fail me.
Insightful musing, confounding my mind
I must look in the mirror, to see me.

No image seen, in the mirror of truth.
I no longer believe in a lie.
Life is a risk, not promised happiness.

One morning a frail scribe was free of pain.
No longer captive, finally at peace.
Mind yearning to melt, through cold, iron bars.

Roaming among birds, breathing in fresh air.
Hearing clandestine debates of viewpoints
music to an old maestro of words, ears.

Confession, fell on deaf ears, matters not.
What was said needed, to be said, cleansing:
will they remember childhood dreams, of old?

This next poem was written during the Rwandan genocide that began in April, 1994. During that same time frame, in Europe another genocide had already begun in 1992 after the dissolution of the country of Yugoslavia. In Rwanda, Hutus were brutally murdering tens of thousands of Tutsis -men, women and children. By the end of that genocide, an estimated 500,000 to one million Tutsis and Hutus had perished. In the late 1970's, up to two million Cambodians brutally died of starvation, disease, forced labor or execution, carried out by a communist dictatorship. Once again we see the human race looking for an excuse to destroy itself.

Like The Lion

Are we like the noble lion, which has an inborn hate for hyenas? Whose scent instinctively drives the lion on a murderous rampage against its **"natural enemy!"**

Death Squads
Death Camps
Killing Fields
Filled with bones
of young and old

Is it acceptable to succumb to monstrous desires?
Rather than struggling to control them, when we have hyenas to hunt? If finding none, have we not made our own?

Bloody tribal rivalries
Rapes, mutilations, massacres
Ethnic cleansing,
Politically correct terminology
for genocide

We could justify that we are eliminating hyenas!
*Or, are we like the lion with a murderous instinct to destroy our **"natural enemy?"***

*Are we, that **"Enemy?"***

    I will close this chapter with one of my early poems. During my lifetime I have witnessed the worst in humanity and in nature. In every decade since 1950, there have been wars, genocides, and famines, devastating nature disasters, worldwide epidemics that have killed and dislocated tens of millions of people.
    During that same time, man has walked on the moon, created and inhabited space stations that orbit the earth, discovered even more lifesaving drugs and medical procedures, aided strangers in need around the world and vanquished an empire that sternly controlled the lives of millions of citizens of many countries. Many were murdered as they tried to escape this harsh reality. Even though darkness begins to emerge at sunset, it cannot, keep the world in darkness, at sunrise.

Canvas World

Sky, grass, flowers painted his landscape.
Running deer, chirping birds, lived in his canvas
world.
Giving birth to and watching his creation mature,
filled him with pride.

A painter well pleased, rested.
Hunters killed his deer, silenced his birds.
Progress concreted over his flowers and grass.
Pollution choked his sky.

Ashamed and sad he had fallen asleep.
The painter started over and never slept again.

Why Did I Serve

John L. Grand
US Army Retired

I am an American, I love my country and I honor our flag with the love and respect that it deserves.

I served my country in the U.S. Army and I have bled for my country! During my service, I earned the *Combat Infantryman's Badge* and I was awarded two *Purple Hearts* for wounds received, 2 *Bronze Stars* for valor and a *Silver Star* for my actions in combat.

From a very young age, I was determined to be a solider. My emotional attachment to our country and our way of life drove me to want to do whatever it took to protect this country, its citizens and our governing body as provided under the *Constitution*.

I firmly believe that our Founding Fathers gave us a method of government that is strong and has united our perspective for 241 years. Although we have only had a total of 22 years of peace in that time, we survived many wars because we are a strong and united country.

My personal mission to this country was comprised of two major motivations:

1) To protect American citizens from our enemies; and

2) To protect our Constitutional Rights and privileges with the understanding that all American Citizens would be treated equally.

Our country is a Republic governed under the Constitutional guidelines established by our Founding Fathers. The Constitution ensures our citizens the right to be treated as equals and it guarantees the right of the people to inform our elected officials when we are dissatisfied with the decisions that they make.

The constitution gave us an opportunity to change governments through the ballot box, every American citizen has to right to vote for the person or persons they feel will uphold our way of life and would govern all American Citizens equally.

We also have a right to protest when the government is doing something to deny, or not doing enough to ensure, the equality of all our citizens.

In the 1960's and 70's many American citizens, who disagreed with our involvement in Vietnam, demonstrated against that war and chose to burn our flag in protest, as an expression of their agitation and opposition.

As an Active Duty member of the U.S. Military, I was very upset and distraught over their disrespect to our flag, a flag that many of my military brothers and sisters in arms fought for and came home under.

The right to their demonstrations and flag burning was brought to the Supreme Court to determine the constitutionality of their actions.

The Supreme Court found that the First Amendment gave our citizens the right to burn the flag as an expression of their freedom of speech and their right to protest. They were protected under the Constitution.

That ruling made me angry, I couldn't believe that American citizens were given a green light to burn our beautiful flag, the symbol of our freedom and unity.

However, after much thought, it gave me pause to question my reasons for being upset. I had to think long and hard, but in the end I had to agree, although I would not burn our flag, others had the right to do so, under the constitution.

Protecting our rights under the Constitution means we have to protect everyone's rights. The Constitution is not an instrument we can cherry pick, to suit only our own personal ideals and emotions. It is plainly written and clearly stated that all American citizens would be protected equally.

Today, many people are denigrating the NFL (National Football League) because, to protest against racial inequality, some NFL players are kneeling during the *National Anthem* and tribute to our flag.

They are not burning the flag. In my mind, kneeling is also a show of respect for the flag and the *National Anthem*. While bringing to the forefront their protest of racial inequality in a peaceful and respectful way, they are exercising their freedom of speech.

Today we have billionaires spending millions of dollars to sway the public to vote for the candidates they want in office. Some would say they are buying seats for those who will be more responsive to their needs, over the needs of the general public.

This seems unfair to the majority of American citizens. However, the Supreme Court has ruled it is their right to spend as much money as they want, without having to reveal where that money came from, as their freedom of speech at work.

What comes to my mind is that in the 1960s and 70s the majority of the protesters who were burning the flag, were white, while the majority of the NFL protesters today are black.

Is that why the flag burners of yesterday were not wrong and they were only practicing their constitutional rights, while the NFL protesters of today are wrong and are denigrated and ridiculed for kneeling to the flag, claiming they are disrespecting our flag.

I think that is hypocrisy at its ugliest and has no place in America.

Also, when did kneeling become a show of disrespect? Don't we kneel when we show love and respect to God? Or are we disrespecting the Lord Our God when we kneel to pay tribute to him when we pray?

What we should be doing, as a nation, is to embrace the reason for the protest, not the method, while doing what we can to close the divide our nation finds itself in today. We have to work together to correct the racial inequality existing in today's society.

Why did I serve my country?

I served to ensure our enemies were neutralized and to protect the constitutional rights of every American Citizen, including their right to protest.

At times I get the impression that some of our citizens forget we are a republic governed as a democracy. We are not a Dictatorship!

We are still a country of the people, governed for the people and by the people of the United States of America.

God bless the United States!

No Worry, No Hurry

Kristy Hopper

Hi. My name is Kristy – and I am addicted to being late.

Anyone who knows me, is well aware I am rarely on time or early. I do try very hard to never be more than a few minutes late to any event - but there have been a few instances of tardiness with severe consequences. Some of these are much to the dismay of my husband. Before Kristy, he happily lived his life with the stern belief that "ten-minutes-early-is-late" and "twenty-minutes-early-is-on-time."

Although I annoy him daily with my willful disregard to deadlines, my most egregious sin was at the start of our honeymoon.

Did you know traveling outside the U.S. requires airport arrival and check-in a minimum of two hours prior to departure?

You mean an hour and a half isn't early enough?

Our trip was delayed an entire day as the airline refused to allow us to check-in late and we had to rebook flights for the following day.

Instead of being upset with me, David was incredibly patient and understanding. Maybe he was in an extra good mood that day, or maybe he just couldn't bring himself to be mad at me in my pitiful state, hyperventilating and sobbing. It all worked out fine. We went on our glorious vacation and had an incredible experience. Ultimately, nothing was spoiled by my lateness. And what I experienced on our travels will stay with me for the rest of my life.

You see, I have been seriously committed to procrastination and being late my entire life. Until something becomes a looming urgent need, I am free to procrastinate and not worry about it. My favorite personal motto is:

"There's nothing to worry about until there is something to worry about."

While honeymooning with David in Jamaica, I was deeply affected by the laid back and care free attitudes of the tropical islanders. I felt like I was home, with people who understood my soul. Once, we were running late to something (most likely my fault) and the taxi driver kindly offered me a local sentiment:

"Here in Jamaica, we say 'No Worry, No Hurry'."

His words were simple, but so comforting to me.

I understand everyone worries a little now and then. As human beings on this planet, challenges will find us. You probably even create challenges for yourself - we all do. Instead of succumbing to self-doubt, try thinking of difficult moments as opportunities to ask, "How can I be kinder to myself and others right now?"

You see, I believe worry is an enemy.

It is a thief in a happy life.

To reveal happiness in our lives, we need to accept life's difficulties and learn to savor the good. But the truth is we often dwell in excessively negative thinking and self-judgment. When we are obsessed with "what if" scenarios, we are not present in the beautiful experience of life unfolding right before us. Worrying steals our time, our emotional and mental energy. It robs us of enjoying the present.

I believe in the adage, "Worry is interest paid on trouble before it becomes due."

Think about how much time you spend fretting about what might happen. Those stressful moments are not only torturous, but they are profoundly unproductive. With each moment wasted in pointless concern, we are neglecting the opportunity to contribute to our own success and the world around us. The hilarious irony about worrying is the vast majority of concerns never even materialize; only a very small percentage of real concerns actualize. All that time and energy wasted, could be redirected into something more valuable and beneficial.

Author Josh Linkner, did the math on it (in *Forbes Magazine*, October 12, 1997):

- The typical person worries for a total of 3 hours per week
- The total is up to 156 hours per year of immobilizing anxiety
- Let's say 5% of the worries actually come true
- That means 148 hours were wasted worrying about stuff that never ends up happening

What if you recaptured the entire 156 hours and spent your days full of energy and free of anxiety? In addition to enjoying life more, you can use that time to create art, learn a new language, get in shape, play with your kids, counsel a friend, or help your community. Instead of the draining act of living in fear, you can be making a difference and advance your life.

But what about the negative things that do end up happening? Even if you set aside 30 hours to deal with real issues once they occur, you still are left with a gift of over 120 hours to pursue your calling. That's 10 hours a month.

There's nothing to worry about, until there is something to worry about. Think about it; the real challenges you end up facing in life, likely weren't even issues you were worried about.

Pulitzer Prize winner Mary Schmich, observed:

> "Don't worry about the future. Or worry, but know that worrying is as effective as trying to solve an algebra equation by chewing bubble gum. The real troubles in your life are apt to be things that never crossed your worried mind, the kind that blindside you at 4 p.m. on some idle Tuesday" (*Chicago Tribune*, June 1, 1997).

It's time to exit the worry-train and embrace the new riches of time and energy that will come as a result of disengaging this burden. Break free from the prison of useless anxiety and sprint toward the activities that will hasten the most progress in your life. You get to choose what you think about, so you might as well make the most and best of your mind.

I have a few rules I use to decide if something warrants my time and energy to worry about:

1. Can I do something about it right now?
2. Can someone else take immediate action?
3. Will someone die or become injured?

If the answers to those three questions are no, I choose not to worry. Instead, I'll ask for forgiveness, and continue working on my hopelessly late game.

3

Embrace your Dream

The human species thinks in metaphors and learns through stories.

Mary Catherine Bateson

I Feel Like a Teenager at the Age of 50

Dr. Awdhesh Singh

I was born in a small village in the state of *Uttar Pradesh* (UP) in Northern India. My father got married when he was merely 18 years old, still studying in the 11th grade. My mother was 16 at the time of her marriage and studied up to the fifth grade only. My father later got admission into a college in *Lucknow* to study civil engineering. By the time he received his diploma, I had a younger brother. We were five brothers and one sister.

My father got a job as a junior engineer in the *UP Irrigation Department*. We stayed in a one room house, having a total area of barely 300 square feet (30 square meters). The house was partitioned in half. We put a florescent light above the partition that illuminated both areas. The roof of the house was made of asbestos sheet that protected us from rain, but hardly protected us from the heat of summer which often reached 46 degrees Celsius (115 degrees F), during May and June.

I was an average student until fifth grade and I was never ranked among the top three students in the class. We moved to *Lucknow* thereafter and my siblings and I were admitted to a school named *Bharat Bharati Montesari School* (BBMS). The school was just across the road from our house and its fees were quite low, which suited my family. I was ranked second in my class from the sixth grade onward.

Transformation started when I got admitted into high school. For the first time in my life, I started enjoying studies, particularly Mathematics and Physics. I would never get tired of solving complex mathematical problems and using my little knowledge of physics to understand the world better.

After two years, I was selected in the most prestigious competitive examination in India, the Joint Entrance Examination (JEE), to study at the *Indian Institute of Technology* (IIT), *Benaras Hindu University* (IIT-BHU) in *Varanasi*.

I graduated in 1987 and got a job at a prestigious company in India. I worked there for a year, but did not like the corporate world. I decided to quit that job to study for a Master's Degree in Engineering at *IIT Delhi*. I took the *Civil Services Examination* (CSE) for the selection of the top Civil Services in India and passed the test in my first attempt. I joined the *Indian Revenue Service* (IRS), *Customs & Central Excise*, in 1991.

Government services are most sought after in India and IRS was one of the most prestigious services in India. My selection made my family proud and my life became quite comfortable. I got married in 1992 and was blessed with two daughters, in 1993 and 1994.

Though I was happy being an IRS officer, the job was becoming monotonous as there was nothing much to learn, or any opportunity to grow intellectually. I had a feeling of stagnation despite getting promotions and appreciations in my job.

We all have some basic traits in us which we often fail to explore due to our quest to achieve worldly successes. I too was following the rat race of the world and doing what the world valued rather than what I valued. I decided to focus on my inner self, get to know myself and search the hidden secrets of the world.

I developed the habit of reading books on self-help, philosophy, religion and spirituality for better understanding of human life. I was able to grasp more complex ideas of philosophers and develop a deeper understanding of the world.

In 2002, I took the next big leap to pursue my passion of learning and decided to study for a Ph.D. in E-Governance from the *Indian Institute of Information Technology and Management* (IIITM), in *Gwalior*. It was the first time that I joined any course of study purely for the love of knowledge as no benefit was to accrue to me in my career due to this degree. Here, I faced the first great challenge of my life.

I was required to publish research papers in international journals and conferences as part of my Ph.D. work. I found the task quite daunting since I had never written even a half-page article during my school and college days. However, with the help of my professors, I learned to carry out research and got seven papers published during my Ph.D. course.

Life is strange and often quite unpredictable. You often discover yourself in a very strange manner. I hated writing papers when I started my Ph.D. program, but after writing serval research papers and submitting my thesis, I found that I actually loved writing. In fact, I developed so much confidence on my writing that I realized that I could easily become a published writer.

I wrote a book entitled in 2005, *Change Your Nature to Change Your Life* within three months of submitting my Ph.D. thesis and sent it to a dozen publishers. However, I was soon to face the bitterest truth of life when all the publishers rejected my book. I was heartbroken with my maiden attempt to become an author. I was, however, confident about my writing as I believed in myself. I often remembered this beautiful poem of Roger Edwardo:

If you think you are beaten, you are;
If you think you dare not, you don't.
If you'd like to win, but you think you can't,
It is almost a certain - you won't.

If you think you'll lose, you've lost;
For out in this world we find
Success begins with a fellow's will
It's all in the state of mind.

If you think you're outclassed, you are;
You've got to think high to rise.
You've got to be sure of yourself before
You can ever win the prize.

Life's battles don't always go
To the stronger or faster man;
But sooner or later the man who wins
Is the one who thinks he can!

    I had made up my mind.
    I was not going to give up my dream to become a published writer. I created my own website *www.scienceofsoul.com* in 2006 and started publishing articles on it. A few months later, I discovered another website *www.ezinearticles.com* which allowed me to write articles that were made

available to internet publishers. I used to write two articles every weekend and thus wrote around 500 articles in the next five year. These articles were republished on several magazines and journals.

I wrote my next book, *Practicing Spiritual Intelligence,* in 2011 and again sent it to a dozen publishers. This time, one publisher, *Wisdom Tree,* agreed to publish my book. We had several rounds of editing and finally my book was released in 2013 and my dream to become a published author was realized. This book was greeted with wide appreciation from readers.

My next book, *The Secret Red book of Leadership,* was released in 2015, followed by my third book, *Myths are Real and Reality is a Myth,* in 2017. That same year, I also wrote the book, *Goods and Services Tax Made Simple.*

As my interest in writing grew, I felt constrained to be in government service. I felt it greatly restricted my freedom of expression. I was also required to ask permission when I left the city or delivered a lecture at any forum. Hence, I took voluntary retirement from the IRS in October 2016 to focus on writing and education.

Meanwhile, in August 2015, I had joined *Quora.com,* an American based question-and-answer website that launched me as a writer worldwide. I started posting answers to different questions on a regular basis. Soon my answers started getting a large number of views and by July 2018, my answer views passed 100 million and I became the fifth most followed *Quora* writer in the world, with over 230,000 followers. I received huge recognition due to *Quora* and I was invited to the top institutes in India for lectures, seminars and *TEDx* talks.

I love to write and to share my knowledge and experiences with the world. My interest in education prompted me to start a *YouTube* channel in 2017 with the name of *Awdhesh Academy,* where I started posting videos of my lectures on subjects such as: 1) life skills, 2) school and 3) professional courses.

I later set up a company, *Awdhesh Classes Private Limited,* and in May 2018 I formally commenced the online teaching platform *www.awdheshacademy.com*. We are hoping to post over 1,000 video lessons on this platform by the end of 2018 for half a dozen courses. I thus started my entrepreneurial journey in 2018, after I turned fifty years old.

I believe that my best is yet to come and my journey of life has just started. I wish to write at least one book every year and post a couple of online courses on the *Academy* every day, besides answering around 1500 questions on *Quora* annually.

I get tremendous joy and satisfaction in writing. I often get messages and emails from readers whose lives were transformed by reading my answers and articles. Their appreciation motivates me to give my best. I strongly believe that I have something valuable to share with the world. Through my books, articles and *Quora* answers, I believe I can inspire many people to lead an improved life through developing a better understanding of the self and the world.

My life is now filled with excitement and hope. I feel like a teenager, full of enough passion, energy and dreams to transform the world.

Urban Boatman:
A Father's Day Memoir

G.L. Smith

While working in an office filing contracts, I would often take a break and stare out of the restroom window at the river and mountains. Sometimes a man would come cruising down the river in a speedboat. He was wearing a sun visor on his forehead and sunglasses. He slowly cruised by in a laid-back fashion during the day, while the rest of us were earning our pay working.

My husband-to-be was working in a lab, washing test tubes to earn some money to join a fraternity, whose colors were yellow and black. He recalls seeing that urban boatman from time to time cruising down the river.

Time passed. We got married and moved to Texas. One day, we decided to rent a canoe at Lake Whitney. We were excited about it, but we had meager knowledge about how to actually operate a canoe. We found ourselves drifting on the lake, as my husband paddled as best as he could. The skies turned gray and we could hear thunder, so we decided to head for home. My husband attempted to paddle onto the shore, but a snake was waiting there to greet us.

We headed to another spot, but it was too muddy. My husband jumped out of the canoe and struggled to get us onto the shore. He told me it would be easier If I got out too, which I did. He encouraged me to help him pull the canoe to shore. As the rains came, we struggled with the canoe and it was then that

I decided that I would never go boating with him again, in this life time. We had mud up to our knees and cleaned up as much as possible to drive home.

Years passed and we moved to Arizona. My husband headed to *Sears* and bought a canoe for $99.00. He and his pals went fishing from time to time until one day the canoe capsized and they had to swim for shore. He decided that perhaps the canoe was not his type of boat, so he traded it in for a motor boat, with the motor in the back.

He did well with that and often took the kids out, with their little life jackets, to go fishing. I cooked the fish that they caught and identified the ones caught by each as I served it. There were smiles all around the table.

Eventually, the children married and had their own little ones, until there were too many to go out in the motor boat. It was traded in for a pontoon boat. Children and grandkids trotted out in their little life jackets to go boating with Grandpa and a grand time was had by all.

My husband's pals were no longer around to go boating so the boat was sold. By and by, he crossed over the Big Pond and made it into Paradise.

Waiting for him in Heaven, was a workroom with a blueprint to build a speedboat, yellow and black paint, and a pole to place a flag in the rear. He got busy and built the speedboat, placed the flag with writing on it at the rear and painted the speedboat yellow and black. He acquired a sun visor and sunglasses and cruised down the Allegheny River in Pennsylvania a happy man.

He acquired the skills to be an excellent urban boatman.

When it was time for me to cross the Big Pond, I headed to my favorite department store, *Gimbels*, and acquired as much candy as possible. It was called "Stolen Heaven" and consisted of a 2-inch square of marshmallow, covered with chocolate, on top was a layer of caramel and on top of that were cashews or pecans. I acquired as much as possible because I planned to have it for breakfast, lunch and dinner. This is Heaven's reward.

As I exited the store with the candy, I decided to take the Allegheny Exit. Never saw that one before. Outside was a wharf and next to it was a yellow and black boat. Smiling at me was my truelove and he said:

"Get in Damn it!"

"Watch your mouth!" I said.

"I am in Paradise now I can say what I want," he replied.

"What took you so long to get here?" he asked.

"Well, I looked for another husband and couldn't find one as ugly as you," I responded. "If you will remember I told you that I did not feel comfortable around really good-looking guys and that was why I chose you."

"Fasten your seat belt and shut your trap, Woman!"

As we cruised the river, we sang songs, as we had done when we traveled across the country in our station wagon. The kids joined in and sang too in those days.

While he was on TDY (Temporary Duty Yonder) for extended periods, I joined the Wives Club

Singers and sang songs under the direction of Mike Richardson, who may have written one song called, *Last Farewell*. It was a *sea shanty* type of song about a sailor who only knows how to work as a sailor, and his truelove's wish to go with him.

Some of the lyrics were:

(Sailor sings to his true love)
I'm going away at eventide,
Across the wide and rolling sea.
(She responds)
I bid you stay, stay here by my side,
And spend a last farewell with me.
(Sailor)
A wandering sea is all I know
But I love you more than words can show.
(Her response)
Build me a boat that can carry two,
We two shall roam,
My love and I.

They sang one song after another, as they cruised down the Allegheny River, to the Monongahela River, and on down to the Ohio River, then to the Mighty Mississippi until they reached the GULF OF MEXICO!

HOT DOG!!!

They cruised around the Gulf and on the way back to the Allegheny River area, they stopped in New Orleans and picked up some of their great food and an abundant supply of Dixie Land Jazz, and headed back, playing that music and chomping away of the fancy donuts and other goodies, along with the *Gimbels* candy.

Now when it is your turn to cross the Big Pond and you are headed to your Paradise. Along the way, you might see a couple coming down a river, wearing sunglasses and sun visors on their heads, in a yellow and black speedboat and hear them playing Dixie Land Jazz. There is a pole in the rear of the boat and attached is a flag that reads: *BOAT BUILT FOR TWO.*

Embracing the Experience

Ken Requard, M.D.

A dead thing can go with the stream, but only a living thing can go against it. - G.K. Chesterton.

Martin Luther King said: *I have a dream.* He embraced his dream. He did not know what the outcome would be.

Do you have a dream? Have you embraced it?

What has kept you from embracing it? Fear of the unknown? Fear of failure? Fear of being uncomfortable?

In 1988, the *Nike* Company was losing money. Their focus on successful champion athletes was not motivating our "couch potato" society. They realized that they would have to inspire people to embrace activity if they were going to sell more athletic gear. The "Just Do It" advertising campaign was born. It told people that they did not have to be a superstar. They just needed to get out and try to do it. The campaign turned the Company around by encouraging the average person to embrace the athletic experience ... regardless of success or failure.

My father liked sports, but worked too hard physically to have the time or energy for sports. I was not very athletic, but I tried many sports. I had watched snow skiers on TV but had never thought about doing it myself.

I grew up in Virginia, which is not known as a mecca for skiing, having only one ski resort when I was young. One could say that if God had wanted Virginians to ski, He would have given them higher mountains and more snow!

One winter a friend talked me into going snow skiing. I did not know that I would fall in love with skiing until I experienced it. At the top of the mountain, you have two choices: try to ski down, or the embarrassing option of sliding down on your butt.

Skiing also requires total concentration or you will be doing a "tree hug" at 30 mph! To ski well, the first thing you learn is that you have to lean forward ... you have to throw yourself down the mountain!

That's commitment.

Embracing the experience requires commitment.

We tend to dislike the word "commitment." It has the "ring" of finality ... a sense of "no turning back." For instance, some people choose to "live together" to avoid the commitment of marriage.

A commitment story:

In 1519, the Spanish explorer Hernando Cortez decided to seize the treasure of the Aztecs. He took 500 soldiers and 100 sailors and landed his 11 ships on the shores of the Yucatan Peninsula. He faced a powerful empire, undefeated for 600 years. Some of his men feared failure and tried to seize some ships to sail back to Cuba.

Cortez got wind of the plot and captured the ringleaders. He wanted to make sure that the remainder of his men were fully committed to his quest for riches, so he did something that seemed insane to his soldiers: Cortez gave the order to burn and sink the ships!

There would be no turning back.

They were fully committed.

They were going to have to embrace the experience with no guarantee of success.

As a child, I wanted to be an artist. I dismissed that dream because I knew that my father would not be supportive. I considered architecture, but at that time many architects were out of work. Sometimes, we dismiss our dreams because we see others failing. Through a series of unanticipated events and much to my surprise, I ended up in Medical School. In retrospect, I realize that I adopted a dream shared by friends rather than pursuing my own.

My experience with the various clinical specialties taught me what I did not want to do. In my last elective course, I finally found a niche that appealed to my love of imagery: Radiology - the interpretation of medical images. I found that there was an "art" to making images of the body.

I had a successful medical career but the artistic itch never went away. In 1984, eight years after Medical School, I took my first art class since High School. For the next 33 years, I pursued art on a part-time basis. I often thought about becoming a full-time artist but I feared the financial hardships. I believed the myth of the "starving artist."

I am now retired from Radiology and fully committed to my art career, but is it too late? I don't think it is too late for me but I did give up a lot of past opportunities because I wasn't willing to embrace my dream. I think some of us who postpone dreams are waiting for some kind of "sign", some outside source of assurance of success.

The artist Chuck Close said: *Amateurs wait for inspiration; professionals show up and go to work*. I would re-phrase this as:

The uncommitted wait for inspiration; the committed show up and go to work.

It takes courage to merely get started. The first brush stroke in painting is like that first lean down the mountain in skiing or the first stroke of the surgeon's scalpel.

I have painted in the studio for years. Recently, I started painting outdoors, known as "Plein Air" painting. It is hard but I am committed to it because having experienced it, I have embraced the value of it.

Embracing the experience means getting out of our comfort zone.

I used to ski in the *Cascade Mountains*. The Cascades are a chain of volcanoes. I recall standing on the top of a mountain in Oregon. I could see volcanoes poking their peaks through a blanket of clouds stretching from Washington to California. Even if I crashed many times skiing that day, it was worth it to just "be there."

It is the same with outdoor painting. Even if the painting effort fails, there is value in just "being there," just embracing the experience. This is similar to athletes who describe being "in the zone." Too often, our society focuses more on final success than on enjoying the moment.

There can be more satisfaction in "doing" than in "being done".

In fact, when we are done, we could say that we are now "out of the zone." Regarding being "in the zone," there is a scene in *Star Wars* where Yoda is teaching the use of "the force" to Luke Skywalker. Yoda becomes frustrated with Luke's failures. When Luke protests that he is "trying", Yoda says: *Do or do not, there is no try.*

I don't think Yoda was criticizing the act of "trying" because Yoda himself was "trying" to teach Luke. In an obtuse way, Yoda was probably saying: Embrace the experience of the force and success will come.

I would phrase it as:

Focus on being in the moment and the outcome will take care of itself.

Yoda would probably agree that there is no doing without trying. Charles Kettering said: *It doesn't matter if you try and try again and fail. It does matter if you try and fail and fail to try again.* Have you ever seen anyone achieve 100% success?

Great skiers frequently fall. There are no surgeons with 0% complication rates. The first Christian missionary from the USA suffered for 7 years before achieving his first convert. I once saw a nationally known artist do a demonstration and scrape off all the paint at the end!

We usually learn more from failure than from success. Malcolm Muggeridge said: *I can say with complete truthfulness that everything I have learned in my seventy-five years in this world, everything that has truly enhanced and enlightened my existence, has been through affliction.*

We will all fail to some degree and failure does bring suffering. The Apostle Paul said: *we glory in our sufferings, because we know that suffering produces perseverance; perseverance, character; and character, hope.* Romans 5:3-4 (NIV).

Embracing the experience means accepting failure and learning from it.

Are you going to fail to lean forward for fear of falling?

What ship are you reluctant to sink in order to commit to your dream?

Are you going to let the difficulties of "doing" stop you from "trying"?

Are you going to embrace "being there" or miss out on that mountain top experience?

Are you going to look at failure as a learning experience?

Or ... is your life going to be a blank canvas?
What new experience will you embrace?

4

Compassion

Too often we underestimate the power of a touch, a smile, a kind word, a listening ear, an honest compliment, or the smallest act of caring, all of which have the potential to turn a life around.

Leo Buscaglia

What if we Humans came with Expiration Dates?

James E. Babcock

As I sit nearby my 84-year-old mother's death bed, my senses are taking in the rhythm of her nebulizer breathing machine as it does its best against her Chronic Obstructive Pulmonary Disease (COPD). I touch Betty Lou Millett's once smooth, warm skin, though it is now cold and dry, like tissue paper. I can see the color of red in her veins as they struggle to still keep a constant flow of blood to her one last, strongest organ, her heart. Conversation is a moot point, as she also battles with Alzheimer's and Dementia...so all one can do is just be there.

From time to time Mom will break away from her rest and open her eyes, and see which one of her surviving children is nearby. Then, after she flashes her awesome smile, she slowly rolls her eyes back and returns to her slumber state. With everyone around her, we're there waiting for someone who has already passed on to come and collect her. This is the process the hospice worker shares with us, for soon our mother will be gone.

Yes, this is indeed "The Circle of Life", for you cannot have Life without Death. But through all the sadness and grief, a simple thought comes forth -- especially since this will be the 3rd death I will have gone through these last two years. So, being the very creative type of soul I am, I could not help but wonder

. . . **"What if we humans <u>knew</u> the date that we expire?"** Would we then live our lives differently, with a better sense of how our lives and our loved ones truly matter to us? Or would greed, envy and hatred be so necessary that we'd continue operating from a sense of LACK?

We survive on an all-inclusive thought. Even when one wants to selflessly share something of themselves, a tiny little ping goes off to the tune of **"Well, what's in it for me?"** This silly, greedy thought can quickly give birth to worry, anger, and even FEAR! We become disturbed when some primal instinct has changed our game plan...changing it from wanting to do something for the benefit of others, to now doing it with the need to *receive* something we want or need! When we engage in such selfish ways, we ruin the original, noble intent of doing something for nothing. So often, our main drive is to get all we can for ourselves . . . but maybe that would change IF we each knew our own expiration date.

It would still be a hard-fought battle for some. For example, I have shared my bathroom with others as they frequently visited my apartment. It's no hardship . . . but then, one day, I reach for the "paper work," only to discover that the once-full roll of toilet paper is almost gone! NOW I sense lack, Wondering how I'll survive if, say, we finally start World War Three and I wind up with no more TP! Yes, I worry about strange things.

Soon this idiotic thinking starts to affect my body, as various chemicals are now bursting forth, causing our famous "Fight or Flight" response to flare up! Oh yeah! I can't make it through this new Millennium without my TP! WHO do I have to fight?

What's that? There's a small mountain of TP rolls just within arm's length? Oh... well... never mind then.

Would we, well, ME at least, be so MATERIALISTIC if we each knew our own expiration date? As is, we can't make it in this world without more STUFF! Remember the late George Carlin's "A Place for My Stuff" skit?

He would start out explaining that he had "stuff." You know, all the things that supposedly made his life more enjoyable? But then comes the idea that, well, maybe it's not ENOUGH stuff! Which then causes Carlin to want and accumulate MORE stuff! Soon, though, he runs into a dilemma. How does he make room for the NEW stuff when he's already overrun with his OLD stuff? It's an old skit, but isn't that the mindset we all have these days? Instead of desiring knowledge, ideas, accomplishments and relationships, we're pursuing "STUFF."

Then there's the envy for OTHER PEOPLE's stuff. Envy is such a dangerous thing. Once this seed is planted, you make up your mind that you'll do anything and everything to get what you and your family needs and "deserve." "Why do THEY have something and I don't? They're no better than me!"

Mind you, this is also a great way to make scapegoats out of people. Blaming *them* for your lot in life. You can even scapegoat your own family. Blaming the wife and kids for needing you to provide for them. Keeping you away from *whatever else* you wanted to do with your life! Maybe knowledge of our own expiration date would keep these thoughts at bay.

What if you're an over-achiever? You engage in a hyper-drive mindset, and mastermind a way to bring in tons of money (and, consequently, tons of STUFF) -- expecting your spouse and children to sing songs of your wonderfulness as a result! Sure, you may have had to *use and abuse* a few people along the way, but you're a WINNER now! And it's ALWAYS going to be that way, right?

But check out the latest hard luck stories of those in Hollywood who rose to the top of their game and were showered with fame and fortune. What happened to them next? All too often, they wind up in a mansion all by themselves because they've burned their bridges, used or ignored those that once loved and cared about them, and generally stepped on people to reach the top. Unfortunately for them, you meet the same people going DOWN the ladder that you did going UP. Maybe knowledge of their own expiration date would have kept things in perspective.

Then there's suicide. Following the "washed-up has-been" cliché, some former celebrities and power brokers choose to martyr themselves before their bank accounts are totally dried up. To keep up the *appearance* of living the great life of a Super Star, even after the income has dried up. More than money, though, their inner reservoir of love, caring and happiness is already EMPTIED. Maybe knowledge of their own expiration date would have reminded them how precious and *short* life already is. There's no need to rush things. We'll all be gone soon enough.

Still, these misguided souls know there will be a huge caravan at their funeral, of those who desire to pay their last respects AND those vultures who want to snatch a last piece of their fame and success. You're never more loved, adored and respected than at your own funeral! And, if you've got a large estate, isn't the deceased best loved for what he leaves behind? Yes, I suppose so.

But here's the whole reason I got on this rant. My Mom left this world with essentially no finances left to pass on to her surviving children. But for me, my Mom, Betty Lou Millett, DID leave me a fortune!

Not of anything you can buy *new stuff* with. Instead, she gave me the greatest gift any mother can give her son: beautiful and wonderful MEMORIES! Memories of everything she had to bestow on me, when I needed her to be there for me. When I almost wound up on the streets, she opened and *reopened* the door of her home to welcome me back in. Kissing my "boo-boos" every time I wound up making mistake after mistake!

But it was her *heart* that was the truest Gold Nugget and her love for me that was her Greatest Treasure! So sure, she too made mistakes. She raised me to be *almost paranoid* every time I chose to rush out into the world, with dreams of fame and fortune dancing in my head. She always told me to watch out for "THEM!" You know -- them *things, persons,* and *places* I should steer far from because she wanted me to be safe. And really, isn't that what all parents want for us?

Only you yourselves can answer that question -- but I can respond with a resounding YES!

My Mom helped me and cared for me with all she had, and I am sure -- on her last day on this Earth -- she waited to say goodbye to me. I was with her in Chandler, Arizona, but had to rush back home to Tucson to pay my rent, or be hit with a late fee. "Sigh." I couldn't pay by credit card, over the phone. I couldn't pay over the Internet. I had to <u>physically hand a check</u> to the apartment complex manager. Welcome to the 21st Century!

I paid the rent, restocked on water and fruit, and made the trip back to my mother. Once there, I was told she was just barely hanging on, so I sat back down at her bedside. With sadness leaking forth, I took her hand and lowered my head. What happened next was the nurse, who was nearby, told me that Mom opened her eyes and smiled one last time and then she was gone.

Actually no one knew she had passed on until my brother tried to test how much oxygen she was taking in with one of those finger readers. The unit didn't give a reading. Then as several persons flooded into the room, we discovered her pulse was gone too. Then, what occurred could only be described as a great Hollywood ending. As many there told me, Mom hung on until she could see me for one last time!

I have now been witness to two other deaths, of friends whom I cherished. I did my darn best to be at their wakes, 'cause today *cremation* seems to be the more common choice for disposing of earthly remains (without overburdening the surviving loved ones with a funeral cost). Not once did I ever make it through a wake without someone passing me a box of tissues, before I flooded the church and washed everyone away!

But never did I ever feel the Love, Pride, and Closure that I did with my Mother, Betty Lou Millett.

Thank you, Lord and our Savior Jesus, for bestowing on my family the finest Lady, Mother and Caregiver five little souls could ever want or need to raise them. Amen.

Oh...and as for the question, **"What if we humans <u>knew</u> the date that we expire?"** It's an interesting *thought exercise*, but I just can't answer it. Every person is a unique individual, with their own individual outlook and responses. IF we each knew how much time we had, we'd each react differently. *Some* people might become more tolerant, well-rounded and sociable. *Others* (especially those with not much time left) would become lazy and despondent. *Some* might become more focused and driven. Still *others* might become frantic and unbalanced, perpetually convinced that they're "behind schedule" and "running out of time!"

Frankly, it would probably be a mess. Sure, it's easy to say "Live each day as if it were your last, because one day it WILL be!" . . . but MAN that sounds *exhausting*! You can only *sprint* for so long. You can only *concentrate* for so long. Muscles weren't built to be *constantly* flexed.

How about this?

Do what you can. Find people to care about. Make time for some fun. Don't sweat the small stuff. Take care of yourself...and don't worry about your "expiration date."

That works for me.

Places in the Heart

Terry Sprouse

The best and most beautiful things in the world cannot be seen or even touched – they must be felt in the heart."
--Helen Keller

My Black Lab, Blackie, is much more than just a dog.

Blackie is my walking companion and she is my best friend.

When I come home from work, Blackie is so happy to see me that she runs circles around me. When I see her wagging her tail like a wind machine and carrying her favorite squeaky-toy rabbit in her mouth, all the stress from my job just melts away.

A few years ago, my mother was in a nursing home, shortly before she passed away. I would take Blackie to visit her. It revitalized her like a shot of adrenalin in the arm.

Blackie would put her head on my mom's leg and wag her tail as my mom patted her head. My mom's face glowed with serenity. Blackie was completely absorbed in her dog duty to provide companionship to my mom.

I learned a lot about compassion from Blackie. Compassion was not something she turns on and off like a water faucet. For her, it is a way of life.

Crazy Driver

The other day, Blackie and I began our usual morning walk around the neighborhood, a ritual that we have done hundreds of times. We knew every step of the way. What could possibly go wrong?

As we approached the church, I heard a car revving its motor. Vrooom! Vrooomr!

Suddenly, a pickup truck barreled around the corner like a runaway freight train. We jumped back.

The driver stopped and yelled out the window, "Stay off the road, eh!"

I saw the hair on Blackie's back rise up.

Blackie is a big and intimidating dog, but, on the inside she is a little tiny Chihuahua. She instinctively runs from danger, just like my wife instinctively runs when she sees a mouse.

I said to the driver, "Hey Speedy Gonzales, I have an idea. How about sharing the road with pedestrians, eh!"

The driver stared at Blackie. Blackie stared back. I tightened my grip on Blackie's collar. Blackie appeared to be preparing to attack the driver, but I knew she was actually planning to run away in the opposite direction.

Finally, the driver gave us the one finger salute and screeched away.

I looked at Blackie with appreciation. Even though she was no great guard dog, I felt safer when Blackie was with me.

Blackie and I continued our solitary trek with a little less spring in our step.

Spot, My Childhood Pet

A few blocks later I saw someone walking two dogs. One was a big brown dog. The other was a short white dog with a long tail. My heart pounded with excitement.

The white dog reminded me of Spot, the pet dog I had as a child. I have fond memories of Spot.

My parents did not like Spot in my room. Some nights I was terrified that somebody was hiding in my closet. I'd wake up my dad and say, "I heard something in my closet."

Dad came in my room, opened the closet and looked around, a ritual he had performed countless times.

"Nope. No one in there," Dad said.

"But, I heard something."

"Go ... to ... sleep." "S-L-E-E-E-P" my dad said in a deep hypnotic voice while slowly waving his fingers.

My dad left the room.

My father's attempt to put me to sleep with a hypnotic trance failed miserably. I had no alternative but to secretly let Spot into my room.

Blackie Never Forgets

As Blackie and I got close to our house, an elderly lady walking a little poodle approached us going the opposite way. When Blackie spotted the lady, her tail started furiously wagging. The lady had white hair and walked very slowly. Blackie thought it was my mom.

Blackie still carries my mother in her heart. As long as Blackie lives on this earth, a part of my mother will still be alive.

At the very core of her being, Blackie knows that the most beautiful things in the world are only felt in the heart.

If you own a dog, I challenge you. Treat her like the noble and kindhearted creation she is.

You will never find a more faithful friend.

Author Biographies

James Babcock

The name is Babcock. James E. Babcock. And I have a license to THRILL! Which is what I hope to continue doing as someone who has grown tired of what passes for Comics today. Just because it sells doesn't make it right. So I continue with my "three" man art group to crank out as many "Madame X Incorporated," "Dyn-A-Mic Tales" and "Hero Verses Foes Comics" as I possibly can. I am a God Fearing man of "58" who's been living in Tucson, Arizona since the age of eight. My art and stories are a big part of how I see what's occurring in our world today and where I fit in. I am handicapped, but I chose not to live the diagnosis of my illness. So I draw, write, and basically have fun chasing after my STAR! Care to take a look?

Webpage: babcockgraphicspress.com.
Email: toons4u@msn.com

Randy Casarez

Randy Casarez was born and raised in Tucson, AZ. Randy still lives in Tucson, and has four college degrees including Master Degree in Accounting. Randy is a public speaker, and self-published author. Randy wrote his first short story in 2011 called the "The Big Ones." A Fictional story about President George W. Bush sleeping with Jimmy Lopez's girlfriend. Randy has followed politics since he was a kid, and he enjoys writing about real politicians in fictional situations. Randy is writing a fictional story about the 2008 presidential election called "Change Is Within You." When Randy is not writing he enjoys going to Toastmasters meetings. It gives him a chance to work on his public speaking skills, and improve on his leadership skills.

Email: randy_casarez@yahoo.com

John Grand

Originally from Hudson, New York, John left home in 1955 to join the United States Army as an enlisted man. During his 9th year in the Army he was accepted in the Army Officer Candidate Program, graduating as a 2nd Lieutenant. John served two tours in Vietnam in the Mechanized Infantry Unit over the period of 1967-1968 and 1969. He retired from the United States Army in 1976 with 21 years of service. After retirement John worked for a contractor to train the Saudi Arabian National Guard in Modern Mechanized Infantry Tactics. In 1994, while still in Saudi Arabia, he became a member Toastmasters International. John currently belongs to three Toastmasters clubs in Tucson, Arizona, his home club Aztec, an advanced club Leaders 1st and a special club he started for U. S. Military Veterans. John currently lives in Green Valley, Arizona with Sylvia, his wife of 36 years.

Email: jgrand5@cox.net

William David Hopper

David Hopper is an electrical engineering alum from the University of Arizona currently pursuing a Master of Organizational Leadership from Northern Arizona University. David is the Building Automation Supervisor at the University of Arizona. David earned his Distinguished Toastmaster award in 2016, the highest honor bestowed to a member of the organization. In 2018, he was elected the serve in District 3 leadership as Catalina Division Director. Outside of work and volunteering, David spends his leisure time traveling and scuba diving with his wife.

Email: whopper@email.arizona.edu

Kristy Hopper

Kristy Hopper is a freelancer at heart; working full time as an engineering admin and part time as a pet sitter. Even before officially joining Toastmasters as a member, she supported her husband and his peers with volunteer activities for over two years. Kristy is the current President of her club, From Pen to Podium Toastmasters, 2018-2019 C4 Area Director, and Chief Editor of District 3's newsletter, Roadrunner. She has many passions and interests: animal care/welfare, graphic design, music, movies, art and books. Outside of work, volunteering and hobbies, Kristy spends her leisure time traveling and scuba diving with her husband.

Email: KristyHopper.TM@gmail.com

LinkedIn:
https://www.linkedin.com/in/kristydhopper

Sally Lanyon

Sally Lanyon grew up in mid-Ohio and is growing older and wiser in Southern Arizona. After a career in aerospace and healthcare, Sally enjoys writing, speaking and community work. She is a past president of the Executive Club of Toastmasters, serves on the board of Literacy Connects and is a faculty member for the RYLA (Rotary Youth Leadership Awards) leadership weekend camp in Prescott, AZ. She co-created The Ohio State University's mascot, Brutus Buckeye, when she was a college junior, and fifty years later co-wrote *The Autobiography of Brutus Buckeye: as Told to His Parents, Sally Lanyon and Ray Bourhis.*

Blog: www.thebututsblog.com
E-mail: sally@thebrutusblog.com

Arthur G. Lohman

Even when you're unaware of having a learning disability, you find ways to learn. In the United States Air Force, Art went from towing aircraft to flying on them as a crewmember. As the loadmaster, he was responsible for the safe on/off loading of the aircraft and the in-flight safety of both cargo and passengers. After leaving the military, he learned a new trade. He completed an electronics course to become an electronics mechanic at Hill Air Force Base, Utah, repairing aircraft instruments and equipment.

He joined Toastmasters International to enhance his communication skills with his superiors and co-workers. In 2005 he successfully completed a 15 month Leadership Development Program. He took classes in management on base as well as at Weber State University. Because of health reasons Art retired in 2006. Although he doesn't consider himself to be a professional writer, he has had several poems published, won several speech contests. And Wrote a play, that was performed in 2014 at the Fall Toastmaster District 3 Conference. As a young football player, he knew that obstacles could only be overcome, by tackling them.

E-mail: a.lohman@cox.net

Ken Requard, M.D.

Ken practiced Radiology from 1977 to 2017 in hospital and outpatient settings. In Radiology, Ken served in roles as Chief Resident, Assistant Professor, Imaging Director, Medical Group Director, Medical Staff President, and hospital board member. He has also been an artist since 1985. He served as President of the Eastern Washington Watercolor Society. His artwork has been accepted in over 50 Juried Shows. He is represented by Pitzer Fine Art of Wemberley, Texas. Ken also teaches the Bible to children with Bible Study

Fellowship, International. He has been a member of Aztec Toastmasters since February 2017, achieving Competent Communicator and Visionary Communicator Level 2 status.

For his artwork, blog, and newsletter, see www.kenrequard.com.

Connections:
Instagram: @kenrequard;
Facebook: Ken Requard Fine Art.
Email: ken@kenrequard.com
Phone: 520-780-1281.

Philip Schultz

Colonel Philip Lewis Schultz, Command Pilot, United States Air Force (retired) has had many careers, starting with six years as a newspaper delivery boy. His education includes, a Bachelor of Science at Drexel College in engineering, and a Master's in Business Administration (MBA) at the USAF Institute of Technology. He worked four years as an industrial engineer before being recalled to active duty as a C-45 Transport pilot. He was in charge of contracting with three major military bases. After 15 years with Equitable Life & Causality Insurance Company, he retired at 65.

Since retirement, he has been active in Reading Seed, One on One Partners, hosting foreign students, AWANA (an international Christian nonprofit organization founded to help "reach kids, equip leaders and change the world for God"), attending Toastmasters & Lions Club meetings, and participation in many other clubs and organizations.

Email: philiplewisschultz@gmail.com

Dr. Awdhesh Singh

Dr. Awdhesh Singh is an author, educator, speaker and a Top Quora Writer in the world. He holds his B. Tech. from IIT-BHU Varanasi and M. Tech. from IIT Delhi. He has done his PhD from ABV-Indian Institute of Information Technology and Management (IIITM), Gwalior.

He joined the Indian Revenue Service (C&CE) in 1991 and served the Government of India for more than 25 years. He received the 'WCO Certificate of Merit' instituted by World Customs Organization (WCO) Brussels, on the International Customs Day 2011 and the 'Presidential Award' by the Government of India on the eve of Republic Day 2015. He took voluntary retirement in October 2016 at the rank of Commissioner of Customs, Excise and Service Tax to pursue his passion in writing and teaching.

He had authored four books viz. "Practicing Spiritual Intelligence" (2013), "The Secret Red Book of Leadership" (2015), 'Myths are Real, Reality is a Myth' (2017) and 'GST Made Simple' (2017). He is the FIFTH MOST followed Writer on Quora.com in the world with more than 230,000 followers. His answers have received more than 100 Million views.

Email: awdhesh@awdheshsingh.com
aksinghirs@yahoo.com

G.L. Smith

G.L. Smith is a former writing instructor for *USAFI* (United States Armed Forces Institute). She taught Freshman English and Rhetoric. Ms. Smith enjoys working with students on creative writing projects.

She collaborated with an interesting class of foreign high school students who revised *Dante's Inferno* and inserted the leaders and villains of their countries in various levels in the underworld, for punishment of their misdeeds.

Email: trailstone@aol.com

Terry Sprouse

Terry Sprouse is a speaker, storyteller, and Lincoln-ologist. Ever since reading Carl Sandburg's "Abraham Lincoln," which fortuitously fell into his hands as a literature-starved Peace Corps Volunteer in Honduras in 1986, he has been captivated and inspired by this legendary figure. Terry now delivers speeches and seminars to groups about Mr. Lincoln's storytelling, periodically turning up on radio or television interview shows. Terry has published five books and is a winner of the *USA Best Book Award*. He adheres to Lincoln's belief that "A story the shortest path between a stranger and a friend."

Webpage: www.TerrySprouse.com
YouTube channel: https://goo.gl/ciXqh6
National Speakers Association page: https://goo.gl/sTGV44
Email: tsx15@hotmail.com

Coming Next Year!

The Keys to Success, Part III

www.ingramcontent.com/pod-product-compliance
Lightning Source LLC
Chambersburg PA
CBHW031204090426
42736CB00009B/783